New Thought Pastels

1913

ELLA WHEELER WILCOX

TABLE OF CONTENTS

A DIALOGUE

MORTAL
The world is full of selfishness and greed.
Lord, I would lave its sin.

SPIRIT
Yea, mortal, earth of thy good help has need.
Go cleanse THYSELF within.

MORTAL
Mine ear is hurt by harsh and evil speech.
I would reform men's ways.

SPIRIT
There is but one convincing way to teach.
Speak THOU but words of praise.

MORTAL
On every hand is wretchedness and grief,
Despondency and fear.
Lord, I would give my fellow men relief.

SPIRIT
Be, then, all hope, all cheer.
MORTAL
Lord, I look outward and grow sick at heart,
Such need of change I see.

SPIRIT
Mortal, look IN. Do thy allotted part,
And leave the rest to ME.

THE WEED

A weed is but an unloved flower!
Go dig, and prune, and guide, and wait,
Until it learns its high estate,
And glorifies some bower.
A weed is but an unloved flower!

All sin is virtue unevolved,
Release the angel from the clod -
Go love thy brother up to God.
Behold each problem solved.
All sin is virtue unevolved.

STRENGTH

Who is the strong? Not he who puts to test
His sinews with the strong and proves the best;
But he who dwells where weaklings congregate,
And never lets his splendid strength abate.

Who is the good? Not he who walks each day
With moral men along the high, clean way;
But he who jostles gilded sin and shame,
Yet will not sell his honour or his name.

Who is the wise? Not he who from the start
With Wisdom's followers has taken part;
But he who looks in Folly's tempting eyes,
And turns away, perceiving her disguise.

Who is serene? Not he who flees his kind,
Some mountain fastness, or some cave to find;
But he who in the city's noisiest scene,
Keeps calm within—he only is serene.

AFFIRM

Body and mind, and spirit, all combine
To make the Creature, human and divine.

Of this great trinity no part deny.
Affirm, affirm, the Great Eternal I.

Affirm the body, beautiful and whole,
The earth-expression of immortal soul.

Affirm the mind, the messenger of the hour,
To speed between thee and the source of power.

Affirm the spirit, the Eternal I -
Of this great trinity no part deny.

THE CHOSEN

They stood before the Angel at the gate;
The Angel asked: 'Why should you enter in?'
One said: 'On earth my place was high and great;'
And one: 'I warned my fellow-men from sin;'
Another: 'I was teacher of the faith;
I scorned my life and lived in love with death.'

And one stood silent. 'Speak!' the Angel said;
'What earthly deed has sent you here to-day?'
'Alas! I did but follow where they led,'
He answered sadly: 'I had lost my way -
So new the country, and so strange my flight;
I only sought for guidance and for light.'

'You have no passport?' 'None,' the answer came.
'I loved the earth, tho' lowly was my lot.
I strove to keep my record free from blame,
And make a heaven about my humble spot.
A narrow life; I see it now, too late;
So, Angel, drive me from the heavenly gate.'

The Angel swung the portal wide and free,
And took the sorrowing stranger by the hand.
'Nay, you alone,' he said, 'shall come with me,
Of all this waiting and insistent band.
Of what God gave, you built your paradise;
Behold your mansion waiting in the skies.'

THE NAMELESS

Unnumbered gods may unremembered die;
A thousand creeds may perish and pass by;
Yet do I lift mine eyes to ONE on high.

Unnamed be HE from whom creation came;
There is no word whereby to speak His name
But petty men have mouthed it into shame.

I lift mine eyes, and with a river's force
My love's full tide goes sweeping on its course
To that supreme and all-embracing Source.

Then back through all those thirsting channels roll
The mighty billows of the Over Soul.
And I am He, the portion and the Whole.

As little streams before the flood-tide flee,
As rivers vanish to become the sea,
The I exists no more, for I AM HE,

THE WORD

Oh, a word is a gem, or a stone, or a song,
Or a flame, or a two-edged sword;
Or a rose in bloom, or a sweet perfume,
Or a drop of gall, is a word.

You may choose your word like a connoisseur,
And polish it up with art,
But the word that sways, and stirs, and stays,
Is the word that comes from the heart.

You may work on your word a thousand weeks,
But it will not glow like one
That all unsought, leaps forth white hot,
When the fountains of feeling run.

You may hammer away on the anvil of thought,
And fashion your word with care,
But unless you are stirred to the depths, that word
Shall die on the empty air.

For the word that comes from the brain alone,
Alone to the brain will speed;
But the word that sways, and stirs, and stays,
Oh! that is the word men heed.

ASSISTANCE

Lean on no mortal, Love, and serve;
(For service is love's complement)
But it was never God's intent,
Your spirit from its path should swerve,
To gain another's point of view.
As well might Jupiter, or Mars
Go seeking help from other stars,
Instead of sweeping ON, as you.
Look to the Great Eternal Cause
And not to any man, for light.
Look in; and learn the wrong, and right,
From your own soul's unwritten laws.
And when you question, or demur,
Let Love be your Interpreter.

CREDULITY

If fallacies come knocking at my door,
I'd rather feed, and shelter full a score,
Than hide behind the black portcullis, doubt,
And run the risk of barring one Truth out.

And if pretension for a time deceive,
And prove me one too ready to believe,
Far less my shame, than if by stubborn act,
I brand as lie, some great colossal Fact.

On my soul's door, the latch-string hangs outside;
Within, the lighted candle. Let me guide
Some errant follies, on their wandering way,
Rather, than Wisdom give no welcoming ray.

CONSCIOUSNESS

God, what a glory, is this consciousness,
Of life on life, that comes to those who seek!
Nor would I, if I might, to others speak,
The fulness of that knowledge. It can bless,
Only the eager souls, that willing, press
Along the mountain passes, to the peak.
Not to the dull, the doubting, or the weak,
Will Truth explain, or Mystery confess.

Not to the curious or impatient soul
That in the start, demands the end be shown,
And at each step, stops waiting for a sign;
But to the tireless toiler toward the goal,
Shall the great miracles of God be known
And life revealed, immortal and divine.

THE STRUCTURE

Upon the wreckage of thy yesterday
Design the structure of to-morrow. Lay
Strong corner stones of purpose, and prepare
Great blocks of wisdom, cut from past despair.
Shape mighty pillars of resolve, to set
Deep in the tear-wet mortar of regret.
Work on with patience. Though thy toil be slow,
Yet day by day the edifice shall grow.
Believe in God—in thine own self believe.
All that thou hast desired thou shalt achieve.

OUR SOULS

Our souls should be vessels receiving
The waters of love for relieving
The sorrows of men.

For here lies the pleasure of living:
In taking God's bounties, and giving
The gifts back again.

THE LAW

When the great universe was wrought
To might and majesty from naught,
The all creative force was -
THOUGHT.

That force is thine. Though desolate
The way may seem, command thy fate.
Send forth thy thought -
Create—CREATE!

KNOWLEDGE

Would you believe in Presences Unseen -
In life beyond this earthly life?
BE STILL: Be stiller yet; and listen. Set the screen
Of silence at the portal of your will.
Relax, and let the world go by unheard.
And seal your lips with some all-sacred word.

Breathe 'God,' in any tongue—it means the same;
LOVE ABSOLUTE: Think, feel, absorb the thought;
Shut out all else; until a subtle flame
(A spark from God's creative centre caught)
Shall permeate your being, and shall glow,
Increasing in its splendour, till, YOU KNOW.

Not in a moment, or an hour, or day
The knowledge comes; the power is far too great,
To win in any desultory way.
No soul is worthy till it learns to wait.
Day after day be patient, then, oh, soul;
Month after month—till, lo! the goal! the goal!

GIVE

Live, and thou shalt receive. Give thoughts of cheer,
Of courage and success, to friend and stranger.
And from a thousand sources, far and near,
Strength will be sent thee in thy hour of danger.

Give words of comfort, of defence, and hope,
To mortals crushed by sorrow and by error.
And though thy feet through shadowy paths may grope,
Thou shalt not walk in loneliness or terror.

Give of thy gold, though small thy portion be.
Gold rusts and shrivels in the hand that keeps it.
It grows in one that opens wide and free.
Who sows his harvest is the one who reaps it.

Give of thy love, nor wait to know the worth
Of what thou lovest; and ask no returning.
And wheresoe'er thy pathway leads on earth,
There thou shalt find the lamp of love-light burning.

PERFECTION

The leaf that ripens only in the sun
Is dull and shrivelled ere its race is run.
The leaf that makes a carnival of death
Must tremble first before the north wind's breath.

The life that neither grief nor burden knows
Is dwarfed in sympathy before its close.
The life that grows majestic with the years
Must taste the bitter tonic found in tears.

FEAR

Fear is the twin of Faith's sworn foe, Distrust.
If one breaks in your heart the other must.

Fear is the open enemy of Good.
It means the God in man misunderstood.

Who walks with Fear adown life's road will meet
His boon companions, Failure and Defeat.

But look the bully boldly in the eyes,
With mien undaunted, and he turns and flies.

THE WAY

Between the finite and the infinite
The missing link of Love has left a void.
Supply the link, and earth with Heaven will join
In one continued chain of endless life.

Hell is wherever Love is not, and Heaven
Is Love's location. No dogmatic creed,
No austere faith based on ignoble fear
Can lead thee into realms of joy and peace.
Unless the humblest creatures on the earth
Are bettered by thy loving sympathy
Think not to find a Paradise beyond.

There is no sudden entrance into Heaven.
Slow is the ascent by the path of Love.

UNDERSTOOD

I value more than I despise
My tendency to sin,
Because it helps me sympathise
With all my tempted kin.

He who has nothing in his soul
That links him to the sod,
Knows not that joy of self-control
Which lifts him up to God.

And I am glad my heart can say,
When others trip and fall
(Although I safely passed that way),
'I understand it all.'

HIS MANSION

There was a thought he hid from all men's eyes,
And by his prudent life and deeds of worth
He left a goodly record upon earth
As one both pure and wise.

But when he reached a dark unsightly door
Beyond the grave, there stood his secret thought.
It was the mansion he had built and brought
To dwell in, on that shore.

EFFECT

An unkind tale was whispered in his ear.
He paused to hear.
His thoughts were food that helped a falsehood thrive,
And keep alive.

Years dawned and died. One day by venom's tongue
His name was stung.
He cried aloud, nor dreamed the lie was spawn
Of thoughts long gone.

Each mental wave we send out from the mind,
Or base, or kind,
Completes its circuit, then with added force
Seeks its own source.

THREE THINGS

Know this, ye restless denizens of earth,
Know this, ye seekers after joy and mirth,
Three things there are, eternal in their worth.

Love, that outreaches to the humblest things;
Work that is glad, in what it does and brings;
And faith that soars upon unwearied wings.

Divine the Powers that on this trio wait.
Supreme their conquest, over Time and Fate.
Love, Work, and Faith—these three alone are great.

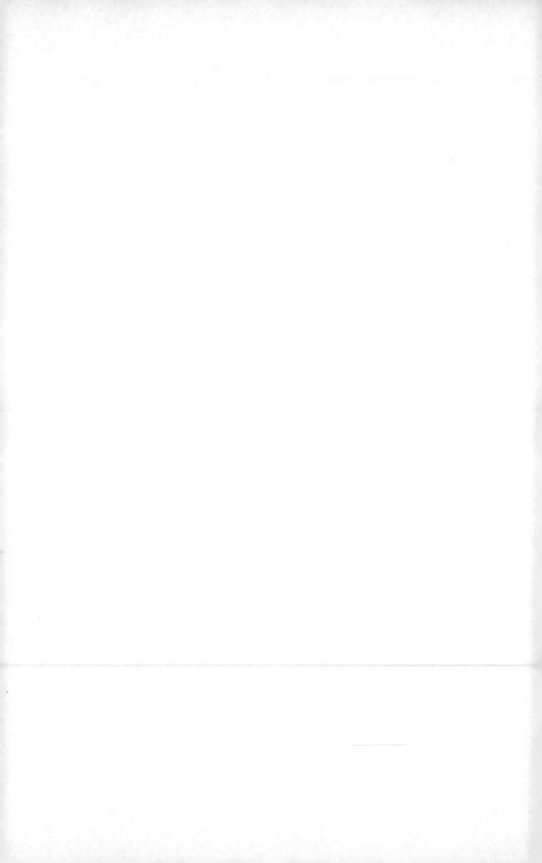

OBSTACLES

'The slothful man saith, There is a lion in the way; a lion is in the street.'—PROVERBS xxvi. 13.

There are no lions in the street;
No lions in the way.
Go seek the goal, thou slothful soul,
Awake, awake, I say.

Thou dost but dream of obstacles;
In God's great lexicon,
That word illstarred, no page has marred;
Press on, I say, press on.

Nothing can keep thee from thine own
But thine own slothful mind.
To one who knocks, each door unlocks;
And he who seeks, shall find.

PRAYER

Lean on thyself until thy strength is tried;
Then ask God's help; it will not be denied.

Use thine own sight to see the way to go;
When darkness falls ask God the path to show.

Think for thyself and reason out thy plan;
God has His work and thou hast thine, oh, man.

Exert thy will and use it for control;
God gave thee jurisdiction of thy soul.

All thine immortal powers bring into play;
Think, act, strive, reason, then look up and pray.

CLIMBING

Who climbs the mountain does not always climb.
The winding road slants downward many a time;
Yet each descent is higher than the last.
Has thy path fallen? That will soon be past.
Beyond the curve the way leads up and on.
Think not thy goal forever lost or gone.
Keep moving forward; if thine aim is right
Thou canst not miss the shining mountain height.
Who would attain to summits still and fair,
Must nerve himself through valleys of despair.

THERE IS NO DEATH, THERE ARE NO DEAD

(Suggested by the book of Mr. Ed. C. Randall.)

'There is no death, there are no dead.'
From zone to zone, from sphere to sphere,
The souls of all who pass from here
By hosts of living thoughts are led;
And dark or bright, those souls must tread
The paths they fashioned year on year.
For hells are built of hate or fear,
And heavens of love our lives have shed.

Across unatlassed worlds of space,
And through God's mighty universe,
With thoughts that bless or thoughts that curse,
Each journeys to his rightful place.
Oh, greater truth no man has said,
'There is no death, there are no dead.'

It lifts the mourner from the sod,
And bids him cast away the reed
Of some uncomforting poor creed,
And walk with Knowledge for a rod.
It bids the doubter seek the broad
Vast fields, where living facts will feed
All those whose patience proves their need
Of these immortal truths of God.

It brings before the eyes of faith

Those realms of radiance, tier on tier,
Where our beloved 'dead' appear,
More beautiful because of 'death.'
It speaks to grief: 'Be comforted;
There is no death, there are no dead.'

REALISATION

Hers was a lonely, shadowed lot;
Or so the unperceiving thought,
Who looked no deeper than her face,
Devoid of chiselled lines of grace -
No farther than her humble grate,
And wondered how she bore her fate.

Yet she was neither lone nor sad;
So much of love her spirit had,
She found an ever-flowing spring
Of happiness in everything.

So near to her was Nature's heart
It seemed a very living part
Of her own self; and bud and blade,
And heat and cold, and sun and shade,
And dawn and sunset, Spring and Fall,
Held raptures for her, one and all.

The year's four changing seasons brought
To her own door what thousands sought
In wandering ways and did not find -
Diversion and content of mind.

She loved the tasks that filled each day -
Such menial duties; but her way
Of looking at them lent a grace
To things the world deemed commonplace.

Obscure and without place or name,
She gloried in another's fame.
Poor, plain and humble in her dress,
She thrilled when beauty and success
And wealth passed by, on pleasure bent;
They made earth seem so opulent.
Yet none of quicker sympathy,
When need or sorrow came, than she,
And so she lived, and so she died.

She woke as from a dream. How wide
And wonderful the avenue
That stretched to her astonished view!
And up the green ascending lawn
A palace caught the rays of dawn.

Then suddenly the silence stirred
With one clear keynote of a bird;
A thousand answered, till ere long
The air was quivering bits of song.
She rose and wandered forth in awe,
Amazed and moved by all she saw,
For, like so many souls who go
Away from earth, she did not know
The cord was severed.

Down the street,
With eager arms stretched forth to greet,
Came one she loved and mourned in youth;
Her mother followed; then the truth
Broke on her, golden wave on wave,
Of knowledge infinite. The grave,
The body and the earthly sphere
Were gone! Immortal life was here!
They led her through the Palace halls;
From gleaming mirrors on the walls
She saw herself, with radiant mien,
And robed in splendour like a queen,
While glory round about her shone.
'All this,' Love murmured, 'is your own.'

And when she gazed with wondering eye,

And questioned whence and where and why,
Love answered thus: 'All Heaven is made
By thoughts on earth; your walls were laid,
Year after year, of purest gold;
The beauty of your mind behold
In this fair palace; ay, and more
Waits farther on, so vast your store.
I was not worthy when I died
To take my place here at your side;
I toiled through long and weary years
From lower planes to these high spheres;
And through the love you sent from earth
I have attained a second birth.
Oft when my erring soul would tire
I felt the strength of your desire;
I heard you breathe my name in prayer,
And courage conquered weak despair.
Ah! earth needs heaven, but heaven indeed
Of earth has just as great a need.'

Across the terrace with a bound
There sped a lambkin and a hound
(Dumb comrades of the old earth land)
And fondled her caressing hand.

YOU LOVED THEM INTO PARADISE

Was answered to her questioning eyes;
'You taught them love; love has no end!
Nor does love's life on form depend.
If there be mortal without love,
He wakes to no new life above.
If love in humbler things exist,
It must through other realms persist
Until all love rays merge in HIM.
Hark! Hear the heavenly Cherubim!'

Then hushed and awed, with joy so vast
It knew no future and no past,
She stood amidst the radiant throng
That came to swell love's welcoming song -
This humble soul from earth's far coast
The centre of the heavenly host.

On earth they see her grave and say:
'She lies there till the judgment day;'
Nor dream, so limited their thought,
What miracles by love are wrought.

9701990R00037

Printed in Great Britain
by Amazon.co.uk, Ltd.,
Marston Gate.